San Diego Public ...
Linda Vista

NOV 22 1999

D0210588

STUNNING

SENTENCES

ALSO BY BRUCE ROSS-LARSON

Edit Yourself
Powerful Paragraphs
Riveting Reports

THE EFFECTIVE WRITING SERIES

STUNNING

SENTENCES

BRUCE ROSS-LARSON

Linda Vista Branch Library
2160 Ulric St.
San Diego, CA 92111

W. W. NORTON & COMPANY • NEW YORK • LONDON

3 1336 04933 1896

Copyright © 1999 by Bruce Ross-Larson

All rights reserved
Printed in the United States of America
First Edition

The text of this book is composed in Electra
with the display set in Futura
Composition by Allentown Digital Services Division of R.R. Donnelly & Sons Company
Manufacturing by the Haddon Craftsmen, Inc.
Book design by JAM Design

Library of Congress Cataloging-in-Publication Data

Ross-Larson, Bruce Clifford, 1942–
    Stunning sentences / Bruce Ross-Larson.
        p.   cm. — (The effective writing series)
    ISBN 0-393-31795-1 (pbk.)
    1. English language — Sentences.   2. English language — Rhetoric.   3. Report
writing.   I. Title.   II. Series: Ross-Larson, Bruce Clifford, 1942–   Effective
writing series.
PE1441.R67   1999
808'.042 — dc21   98-35262
                                                                            CIP

W. W. Norton & Company, Inc., 500 Fifth Avenue, New York, N.Y. 10110
www.wwnorton.com

W. W. Norton & Company Ltd., 10 Coptic Street, London WC1A 1PU

1   2   3   4   5   6   7   8   9   0

For Veruschka
and all my colleagues at the
American Writing Institute

CONTENTS

AUTHOR'S NOTE

The dozens of sentence patterns that I've identified in the main part of this little book are a start, not a finish. Nor do I delve into the word choices and ideas so important for making sentences truly stunning. And the focus is on expository writing, not fiction.

If you run across exemplars of the structures identified here — or find interesting variants, indeed new species—please send them to me at bruce@cdinet.com or browse into www.cdinet. com/AmericanWritingInstitute. I'll try to plug them into the next edition.

I'd like to acknowledge the contributions of my colleagues at the American Writing Institute: Amy Cracknell, Andrea Brunholzl, Jessica Moore, Erika Schelble, Kelli Ashley, Alison Smith, and the interns Brendan McCarthy, Adam Calderon, Jessica Henig, and Ana Dahlman. I'd also like to acknowledge those of my editorial colleagues at Communications Development who reviewed the manuscript throughout its many stages: Meta de Coquereaumont, Alison Strong, Paul Holtz, Daphne Levitas, and Heidi Gifford. And I'd like to thank Clive Crook and Michiko Kakutani for their permission to use the pieces I've attached at the back as well as the many writers whose individual sentences I've used as examples.

BRUCE ROSS-LARSON
Washington, D.C.

STUNNING

SENTENCES

AN APPROACH TO SENTENCES

MOST people use three or four basic sentence constructions—
the simple, compound, and complex sentences taught in all
composition books.

> I came to New York to write.
> *(simple = one independent clause)*

> I came to New York to write, but it took decades
> to find a publisher.
> *(compound = two independent clauses)*

> Because I was naïve and optimistic, I came to
> New York to write.
> *(complex = one dependent clause and one independent)*

> I came to New York, which is a font of inspiration for
> artists of all types, to write.
> *(also complex = one independent clause and one dependent)*

What most people do to give their sentences (their dunning)
variety is merely to multiply their subjects, verbs, objects, complements, phrases, even clauses:

Because I was naïve and optimistic, because I wanted to make a dent on literature, and because I needed a change in the direction of my life, I came to New York, which is a font of inspiration for artists of all types, to taste reality, to test limits, to write about both, and to hope for recognition.

Grammatically correct, but . . .

How do you get from the common to the stunning? Not by diagramming sentences, though that's a good start toward understanding a sentence's pieces. And certainly not by viewing sentences as simple, compound, or complex. I tried both, neither leading me to understand how good writers use sentence structures to make their writing sing. It was only when I began trying to identify what was unusual about a sentence—a dramatic flourish, an elegant repetition, a conversational injection—that I began to see the patterns I've classified here.

So, to move from the common to the stunning, begin to look for patterns in good writing that you can emulate. The idea is to build an arsenal of patterns that take you beyond the common. Careful composition of each sentence may seem painstaking, but it is fundamental to developing an individual style. In a single sentence you can convey tone, style, and message. But follow the dictum that spare use of the uncommon is superior to frequent use, which can quickly careen into cliché.

Think about length. There's nothing wrong with the occasional long, decorative sentence (here named the cascade), so long as it is well crafted. But few people today have the patience or the talent to craft a long sentence well—most only stuff their sentences with extraneous detail. What's long? Anything more than about twenty-five words, or about two lines of typescript. (I once had the pleasure of editing a three-page sentence by Buckminster Fuller.) The test I put to writers is to read a long sentence aloud. If they stumble, if they gasp for air, the sentence is not well crafted, and the stumbles and gasps show them where to make repairs.

It's important to scrutinize every word, phrase, and clause — to see whether you can cut it to give you a sentence that conveys the same meaning more swiftly. Many of the patterns classified here do just that. The fragment. The deft connection. The stark attachment. The occasional short form. Indeed, much of the editing I do is merely drawing lines through words that clutter a sentence but contribute nothing.

Her novels registered these events most secretly, and her letters registered these events not at all.

Her novels registered these events most secretly, her letters not at all.

For guidance on specific ways to trim the fat from your sentences or to break them into shorter, more digestible bits, see another of my little books, *Edit Yourself* (Norton, 1996).

Think about where you put each of a sentence's building blocks — each word, phrase, clause. Add a dash, as I did in the preceding sentence, to set apart a block of words. In the workshops I conduct, I urge people to try to begin separating the movable from the immovable. The subject, verb, and object or complement are usually in a fixed order (usually, because they can sometimes be inverted, to good effect). But the embellishments of prepositional phrases, the complications of *that* and *which* clauses, the conditioning by *if* and *when* clauses — these, you can move. And you should try them at different places in the sentence to see where they have the best effect. Generally, the earlier a word or phrase appears, the greater the emphasis. Apply this maxim for occasional drama.

Propagandist, moralist, prophet — this is the rising sequence.

A sentence's last word or phrase can also be emphatic.

At least two-thirds of us are just plain rich compared to all the rest of the human family—rich in food, rich in clothes, rich in entertainment and amusement, rich in leisure, rich.

The point is: don't give that emphasis away unnecessarily. Choose the word you want to start with—participles often work well.

Americans, having been struck by an annual outbreak of filial sentiment, make more long-distance calls on Mother's Day than on any other day of the year.

Struck by an annual outbreak of filial sentiment, Americans make more long-distance calls on Mother's Day than on any other day of the year.

And think about balance, to create the soothing rhythms and compelling cadences that give your sentences pace. Trimming a sentence's fat helps in this. So does moving a sentence's parts to their most felicitous places. But the balance that comes from re-peated parts, often in parallel constructions, and from recasts, re-versals, and cascades is perhaps most elusive. The reason? You're not simply cutting or moving things. You're revising them, in-venting them. And that takes more thought.

As one wag put it: "Writing? Easiest thing in the world. Just stare at a blank sheet of paper and wait for the drops of blood to form on your forehead." The hope here is that those drops be-come mere sweat, and that by asking the occasional question, in-jecting the occasional short form, making the occasional deft connection, you will become more satisfied with your writing. And so will those reading it.

1

COMMON FORMS

MOST sentences should convey one idea—or two closely related ideas. That generally takes twenty to twenty-five words. The core of the sentence—sometimes all of the sentence—is the main clause. Embellishing this core are modifying phrases and clauses—the prepositional, the defining. Complicating this embellished core are qualifying clauses—the commenting, the conditional. And then there are the multiplier effects of having two or more subjects, verbs, objects, complements, phrases, clauses.

The purpose here is not to classify sentences in the usual less-than-useful ways (simple, compound, complex, compound-complex), but to give you models to (occasionally) emulate as you drive your reader through your paragraphs.

The common forms in this first section make up the full tool kit of structures for most writers. They are fine for basic purposes—but strung together they can be dunning. Variants in the later sections can relieve their relentlessness, giving your writing energy and pace.

The keys to common forms? Keep them clean by trimming as much fat as you can. Inject them with energy by using powerful words. Pick up their pace and cadence by trying to move phrases and clauses to different places in the sentence. (For more on standard edits, see *Edit Yourself*, Norton, 1996.)

DIRECT

Simplest, and thus clearest, the direct sentence has one main clause and is the starting point for countless variants.

> Smart eateries are putting peculiar mushrooms on the menu. *Hard to get more direct than this: who is doing what to what and where.*

> Intimidatingly rakish men in blue blazers smoke cigars and sigh about marrying too young.

> The collapse of an important country's banking system could produce a domino effect.

> It is easy to forget how ubiquitous poetry once was, and how central to human life.

EMBELLISHED

The first common variant to the direct sentence is to attach a phrase—at the front, middle, or end.

> *By all these means,* Alabama has made itself more like the rest of America.
> > *The opening* By all these means *ties this sentence to its predecessors' presumed enumeration of the individual means.*

With his good hand, he worked at the church as a handyman and janitor—among his first English words were "vacuum cleaner."

Part of the problem may be that the administration, *in its zeal to uncover precise chains of command within the apartheid machine,* has been chasing an impossible target.

The multi-storey pagoda came to Japan from China in the sixth century, *with the introduction of Buddhism.*

COMPLICATED

The second common variant to the direct sentence is to add a comment or definition by means of a *which* clause.

> The book also suffers more than usual from Elshtain's prose style, *which is earnest at best and plodding at worst.*
> *Set off by commas, the* which *clause can be left out without disrupting the meaning of the main clause.*

His future, *which initially appeared to be circumscribed by poverty and ignorance,* was drastically altered when he entered primary school.

Users include the local reindeer, *which are said to become drunk and disorderly after feasting on the mushrooms.*

Software firms *that had not existed two years earlier,* such as CyberCash, Yahoo, Spyglass, Spry and Ubique, commanded huge sums as they went public or were bought by established firms.

A that *clause, by contrast, defines a noun and thus is not set off by punctuation.*

CONDITIONED

In addition to embellishing or complicating the main clause, you can condition it with another clause beginning with *when, if, because, since, as,* and their many colleagues.

> *When Mr Clinton toasts Mr Jiang at the White House next week,* there will be no shortage of critics to accuse him of supping with the devil.
> > *The* when *clause tells us when there will be no shortage of critics.*

> Art museums were stodgy places until 1958, *when Frank Lloyd Wright plopped a concrete cupcake on New York's Fifth Avenue.*

> *If these were to shrink,* all would suffer.

> The court refused to suppress the video and sound tapes of the Berger search *because the Constitution forbids censorship even of ill-gotten information.*

> *Since Europe opened its skies to competition last spring,* new little airlines have been taking wing.

> *As evolution goes,* from cave to restaurant is not a huge leap.

MULTIPLIED

Another variant is to combine the foregoing structures and to multiply their parts.

The number of men who consider working women to be worse mothers has dropped precipitously since 1970, but *the number of women* who think so has dropped far less sharply.
Two main clauses joined by but.

They can make excellent eating, but *they can* also kill you.

Collective religious identity is further weakened and *individual religious autonomy further strengthened* by the separation of religion and nationality in American culture—the fact that an American may be of any religion or none and still be fully an American.

She rejected the traditional idea that women and men occupy separate spheres, in which women are naturally passive and men aggressive, and *she challenged* laws treating men and women differently, especially those designed to protect "the weaker sex."

2

OCCASIONAL SHORT FORMS

IF you do a word count of your sentences, you'll find some running thirty, forty, fifty words—too many for today's impatient reader to grasp. And I suspect you'll find only a few running ten to twenty words. Yet shorter sentences can give readers a bit of relief and draw attention to their unencumbered content.

FRAGMENTS

Sentence fragments, disallowed by rigid writers and grousing grammarians, often mimic speech and thus pick up the pace of your writing. Unexpected, they command attention, so you should draw that attention to big points and comments.

> All the crusading doesn't reassure the public. *Just the opposite.*
>> *The full sentence would have been:* Instead, it does just the opposite. *Stripping the first three words from the front and leaving the fragment drives the reader straight to the point.*

And on and on, line by line by line. The range of reference is staggering.

What users have in mind instead is a half-way house in which information is held and often processed on large, shared machines, but viewed and used on personal ones, and accessed via an open network that encourages all the collaboration, communication and information-sharing that management theorists hold so dear. *In a word, the Internet.*

Crash. Stockmarket bulls can act as brave as they like but they cannot deny the terror that this simple word strikes in their breasts.

TO START A PARAGRAPH OR POINT

Try giving your reader some relief with a five- or ten-word sentence. Like the fragment, it attracts attention. So, use it to open an argument. One of the strongest positions for the short sentence is at the beginning of a paragraph.

Documentary films are a worry. First of all, there's the term "documentary" itself, which was thought clumsy by the very man who invented it, John Grierson.
This short, provocative sentence prompts the reader to ask, Why?

It is quite an achievement. Though Boris Yeltsin is erratic in temperament and unsound in body, and though he had presided over a period of change in which most Russians have grown poorer, they have re-elected him.

Greenpeace used no half-measures. Claiming that old growth forests and many species of wild life were being wiped out, it called for all clear-cutting to stop, and no more new forest roads.

But others aren't so sure. "We have yet to find evidence that the introduction of new technology in schools raises test scores," says the Abell Foundation's Kate Walsh. Even some advocates, like consultant Margaret Riel, concede that test scores don't prove the case for computer networking.

TO FINISH A PARAGRAPH OR POINT

Finish a paragraph with a short declarative sentence to reinforce your point, put it in a broad perspective, or create a bridge to the next paragraph. You can also inject a bit of your humorous or skeptical self.

Ordinary people may not dine in three-star restaurants, but they have enough to eat; they may not wear Bruno Maglis, but they do not go barefoot; they may not live in Malibu, but they have roofs over their heads. *Yet it was not always thus.*
Here, the writer is setting up the coming paragraph.

It's not that publishers are irrational or corrupt. *They're just cursed.*

But this tale of two schools shows that it is possible for poor, inner-city children to get a good education in an orderly and happy school. The things that seem to matter—good management, well-designed lessons, careful planning and high expectations—are harder to achieve than simply throwing money at schools or cutting class sizes. *But it can be done.*

It's not hard to find the winner in the Sudanese war, or in any war in Africa: it is the microbes that always emerge victorious. *Infectious disease flowers in conditions of anarchy.*

PAIRS AND TRIOS

Two or more short sentences add cadence. They also separate ideas that would otherwise be more closely linked by a conjunction in a single sentence.

Literature is invention. Fiction is fiction. To call a story a true story is an insult to both art and truth.
> *The period after invention stops the reader momentarily, abruptly separating what follows. Compare the effect with:* Literature is invention, and fiction is fiction. *Far less clear that you're dealing with two separate ideas, not two linked ones.*

Busy on two phones at once trying to stem disaster, you had no time to turn and look. *You didn't need to. You felt him.*

We detest both words. We spit them at each other with the fury of hissing geese. *We duck and dodge them.*

I came. I saw. I conquered.
> *Of course, Cicero's tricolon for Caesar.*

3

DRAMATIC FLOURISHES

AN array of flourishes can add drama to what otherwise would be common. They range from unusual punctuation, to draw attention to a word or phrase, to unusual word orders.

INTERRUPTIVE DASHES

You can occasionally use a dash to separate part of a sentence and thus draw attention to it, just as you would with a dramatic pause in speech. The dash forces your readers to momentarily reflect on what precedes the dash—and then flings them into what follows.

> New York is a city ripe with extremes—of wealth and poverty, of creative energy and rage.
> *Without the dash, the reader would have trouble disentangling* with extremes of wealth *from* of wealth and poverty. *With it,* city ripe with extremes *is clearly articulated from the elaborations:* of wealth and poverty, of creative energy and rage.

So there's the mess—to date.

The vagabonds went on to Cuzco, an ancient city—or, rather, two or three different cities piled one on top of another.

Although Kuusisto's love for poetry can result in patches of overly self-conscious prose—"my soul crawls around like a snail exploring a piece of broken glass"—he is a powerful writer with a musical ear for language and a gift for emotional candor.

IMPERATIVES

Using the imperative is like voicing a command. Spare use grabs attention. Overuse slides into the dictatorial.

Add a bit of Iraqi intransigence, *subtract* a bit of Russian inge-nuity, *throw in* a bit of UN Security Council discord, and the choice for America would have been, broadly, acquiescence or air strikes.

> *Here, the writer is asking us to act. The result: we as readers take far more note of* intransigence, ingenuity, *and* discord *than we would in the prepositional blur of* Given the com-bination of Iraqi intransigence, Russian ingenuity, and UN Security Council discord, ...

Trek to the tops of mountains, the sources of rivers, the earth's icebound poles.

Never mind that these charges usually evaporate under scrutiny: much of the software world is convinced that Microsoft simply does not play fair.

In Europe, where banks have long had a foot in both camps, the trading one is getting bigger: *witness* the unseemly rush by

Swiss and German bankers to lay their hands on medium-sized British merchant banks with large trading outfits.

DIRECT ADDRESS

Addressing your readers, as I do throughout this little book, can make your writing more conversational and thus more personal.

If *your* stocks have risen so much in recent years that they represent an uncomfortably large portion of *your* assets, *you* should consider long-term U.S. Treasury bonds.
The personal pronouns your *and* you *draw the reader into the sentence far more than would the impersonal:* If stocks have risen so much in recent years that they represent an uncomfortably large portion of an individual's assets, one should consider long-term U.S. Treasury bonds. *Compare the effect of writing* you should consider *with that of writing simply* consider, *the difference between direct address and the imperative.*

We know *you're* reading this.

Turn off a main road, wander into a village, go to see an ancient ruin, and *you* are in another country, the one where people live as they have for so many thousands of years.
See how the imperatives are softened?

And *you*, with *your* western products, training, cash, clout and back-up, are fortunate compared with *your* local counterparts.

RECASTS

The recast takes the general and makes it more specific, adding power and clarity that neither could achieve on its own. Some recasts are elaborations, others definitions, still others transformations. Note that most of them are stark attachments (pages 54–57), a signal of the link between the specific and the general.

In the past plagues were often marked by their lack of discrimination, *by the way in which they laid low vast swaths of the population with little regard for station or wealth or sex or religion.*

The second by might *send the reader on the wrong track of thinking that a third by* might *be coming to complete a series and that what follows the second by is launching something different, not similar. By sentence's end, however, it is obvious that the second by is a stark attachment, making more concrete the abstract* lack of discrimination.

Unbelief remains omnipresent in American life, *the position one takes by taking no position.*

Part of it was sheer recklessness, *a determination to plunge ahead, regardless of cars and walls and stairs.*

Collective religious identity is further weakened and individual religious autonomy further strengthened by the separation of religion and nationality in American culture—*the fact that an American may be of any religion or none and still be fully an American.*

REVERSALS

The reversal adds to the power of what you mean by stating the same idea negatively and then positively, or sometimes vice versa. The negative to positive is stronger because it sets up an expectation.

Medical expenditures used to be small, not because doctors were cheap or hospitals were well managed but because there was only so much medicine had to offer, no matter how much you were willing to spend.

Two competing causes, and the writer tells you which is not the real one and which is, starting with the negative. Imagine the order reversed—and the loss of suspense.

The trouble is not with the facts. The trouble is that clear and honest inferences have not been drawn from the facts.

It's not so much that Wallace thinks about politics all the time as that she is continually registering its consequences on the lives of all the people she knows.

It is not that problems are not solved and questions not answered, but every solved problem generates dozens of new ones and the process gives no sign of ending.

INVERSIONS

The inversion changes common sentence order to shift a word or group of words to the emphatic opening slot and to add cadence.

So common is the experience of violent crime there that it has specialized trauma clinics for victims.

Inverting the common order for The experience of violent crime is so common there . . . *puts* so common *in front, giving it far more emphasis, and rightly submerges the flat* The experience of. . . .

Only in Asia are the Japanese doing well.

Only in the virtual world of her fiction could Austen assert control.

Nowhere is this clearer than in the world of art, where adversarial and subversive impulses have long been equated with daring and creativity.

CASCADES

The literati of the *New York Times Book Review,* seldom reined in by the short declarative sentence, often suffuse their reviews with colors, images, and sounds missing in most expository writing. So, to prove that not all your sentences need be short, here are some long ones.

So this language, with its echoes of nomads and emperors, pashas and *ghazis,* sultans and riches, and country matters, with its verbs of more than forty tenses, including the very useful one for innuendo that I wish we had, its oblique politenesses, this language with its own poetry of front- and back-rhyming vowels, this old tongue that contains within it all the past of Anatolia, is, for me, a shorthand.
The repetition of this language *and the recast as* this old tongue *embrace, indeed contain and make more apparent, the cascade of* with its echoes, with its verbs, its oblique politenesses, *and* with its own poetry.

Ulysses is the description of a single day, the sixteenth of June 1904, a Thursday, a day in the mingled and separate lives of a number of characters walking, riding, sitting, talking, dreaming, drinking, and going through a number of minor and major physiological and philosophical actions during this one day in Dublin and the early morning hours of the next day.

Whether naturalists or cowboys, whether bluegrass aristocrats or racetrack touts, whether distinguished academics or little girls gone horse-crazy, all readers with an interest in these large, remarkable animals are bound to be fascinated by Budiansky's knowledge, by his original thinking, by the authority with which he says what many other scientists lack the wisdom or the courage to say, and by the ferocity and tenderness of his voice.

He'd been just as deeply engaged by the challenge of rocks, for instance—scouring quarries throughout the country before settling on green chert from the California Gold Country for the boulders at the head of the stream, Montana Kinnesaw for the flanks of the watercourse, clean-cut slabs of Tennessee Blue Ridge sandstone for the footpaths, and carnelian granite from South Dakota for the staggered waterfall.

FIRST AND LAST

First and last—the two parts of sentences that are most emphatic. (My first draft of this sentence was *The first and last parts of sentences are the most emphatic, the last usually the most.*) That is why it pays to see whether you can change the common order to draw attention to more important words.

Wings, legs, lungs: all were revolutionary mutations once.
Stacking words at the front of a sentence, abruptly attaching
them to their pronoun with a colon or dash, sets them off more
starkly than does running them in.

Propagandist, moralist, prophet — this is the rising sequence.

At least two-thirds of us are just plain rich compared to all the
rest of the human family — rich in food, rich in clothes, rich in
entertainment and amusement, rich in leisure, *rich.*
Imagine this without the exclamatory rich *standing alone at*
the end.

He reached for a word that expressed "shame, disgrace, evil
reputation, obloquy, opprobrium." His choice: *infamy.*

EXCLAMATIONS

Exclamations are stand-alone words or sentences that are often
followed by exclamation points. Reserve exclamations for highly
expressive moments — to convey humor, disgust, or exuberance.

Several years ago a scientific journal published instructions
for building a nuclear bomb. Where? *On paper!*
This is from a satirical essay about paper, not the Internet, as
a dangerous medium. The exclamation "On paper!" shouts at
the reader, magnifying the irony of paper's danger. Imagine it
without the exclamation point.

It will take shape, as all civilizations take shape, by the living
of it, by work and effort, by trial and error, by enterprise and adventure and experience. *And by imagination!*

A cane with a shrunken human head for a handle!

Oops. There were already two Whistling Pig microbrews on the market.

INTERJECTIONS

With interjections, writers speak to the reader and themselves. Like exclamations, interjections are often followed by exclamation points. Unlike exclamations, they do not stand alone but are part of a sentence, though not grammatically tied to it.

> *Ah, yes,* mere adultery (mundane, commonplace and in divorce, mostly a legal irrelevancy) has ended yet another military career.
> *Added to the regret of* Ah *is the resignation of* yes.

> It goes: *gosh,* isn't Motorola amazing, all those cell phones it sells, all that total quality, all that training—*gee,* whadda company!

> *Ah,* this getting older, however fortunate one's circumstances, is a scary business.

> He is—*and how old-fashioned the words sound!*—something more than that, something resolutely indefinable, unpredictable.

HIGHLIGHTS

Italics or quotation marks can highlight a word or phrase used ironically or in an otherwise unconventional way.

Another form of diversification, *bancassurance* — tie-ups between banks and insurance companies — is still all the rage in Europe too.

    Italics often signal a foreign word, until it is common in English.

We are very reserved, for we have been warned not to act "green," that the city people can spot a "sucker" a mile away.

Nevertheless the simple statement stands: we are *in* the war. The irony is that Hitler knows it — and most Americans don't.

    Italics can stress a word, as if in speech.

The second comes from Vice-President Al Gore in 1992: "Scientists concluded — *almost unanimously* — that global warming is real and the time to act is now." (The italics are ours.)

    Some writers use italics to highlight words in quoted material, adding a parenthetical — "(italics mine)" — or similar notation.

4

ELEGANT REPETITIONS

REPETITION —far too often avoided—can be a powerful rhetorical device. It can bring order and balance to a sentence's parts. And it can rivet a word to the reader's frontal lobe with more impact than elegant variation ever could.

WORD

Repeating a word increases its power in the sentence by forcing the reader to reconsider its meaning and that of the words that it frames or modifies.

> However, let us not confuse the physical eye, that *monstrous* masterpiece of evolution, with the mind, an even more *monstrous* achievement.
>
> *Adding the wonderful* monstrous *transforms the meaning of* masterpiece, *and repeating it before* achievement *sets off the contrast between* eye *and* mind *and more than doubles its power in the sentence.*

In this whole matter of War and Peace especially, we have been at *various* times and in *various* ways *false* to ourselves, *false* to each other, *false* to the facts of history and *false* to the future.

Chinatown is *ghetto*, my friends are *ghetto*, I am *ghetto*.

Already in the pace of the town, I strolled *slowly*, *slowly*, up the great wide ramp over the first fosse, once a moat, that day a long slope covered with flowers.
> *Note with the second* slowly *the tendency to read it more slowly, to stretch it out.*

ROOT

Repeating the root of a word is a way to signal different meaning and to link two ideas more strongly than would occur otherwise. Because the reader must slow down to register and consider the link, be sure you're not just being cute.

Far from discrediting liberalism, corruption is discredited by it.
> *A nice turn—from* discrediting *to* discredited.

It was a dramatic, not to say melodramatic, story.

Whatever it was, it caused 96% of marine species to *disappear* and dinosaurs to *appear*.

Book or music or painting, play or film, what arrests us and awes us is the realization that the *inexpressible* is arising from what is being *expressed*.

PREFIX OR SUFFIX

Repeating a prefix or suffix does more than show that words are doing the same work in a sentence. It forces the reader to see their association. This gives sentences cadence and pace.

> Blind*ly*, unintentional*ly*, accidental*ly* and real*ly* in spite of ourselves, we are already a world power in all the trivial ways— in very human ways.

> Common sense is fundamentally *im*moral, for the natural morals of mankind are as irrational as the magic rites that they evolved since the *im*memorial dimness of time.

> Characters and authority figures pop into the story *un*announced and *un*explained.

> Acts of char*ity* usually have about them a whiff of sanct*ity*.

PREPOSITION

A special case of repeating a word, a repeated preposition separates what otherwise would be the many objects of one preposition, emphasizing that they are more separate than joined. It also throws more emphasis on the preposition.

> No longer do our lives depend upon the soil, the sun, the rain, or the wind; we live *by* the grace of jobs and *by* the brutal logic of jobs.
>> *In the first series, the emphasis goes to the objects* soil, sun, rain, *and* wind, *while* upon *is forgotten. In the second,* by *pulls the emphasis to* by the grace of jobs *and* by the brutal logic of jobs.

Much more could be said *in* amplification, *in* qualification, and *in* argument.

To the storyteller we turn *for* entertainment, *for* mental excitement of the simplest kind, *for* emotional participation, *for* the pleasure of traveling in some remote region in space or time.

She has an instinctive politician's gift of connecting—*to* women, *to* men, *to* old people, *to* teenagers, *to* the guy in the Staten Island deli who took her order the other weekend after she finished a five-mile run.

SOUND

Alliteration, the repetition of a sound at the beginning of two or more words in a sentence, can add poetry to the ordinary. Like all repetition, it strengthens the link between words and the attention to those linked words.

> Does the *quaint quality* of *quondam* make you *quiver?*
> *How can you not see first the pairing of* quaint *and* quality
> *and then tie them to* quondam *(whatever that means: but I'll
> bet you look it up), given the last repetition in* quiver.

Fatter capital ratios, *fancy* risk-management systems and *faster* diversification: all of these things are undoubtedly creating a *fitter* banking system.

"Baywatch," that inane *cavalcade* of *cavorting California* hunks and babes, was initially canceled after one season on NBC, but it has gone on to be seen by more people on the planet than any other entertainment show in history.

The last *leave* of *thee* takes my *weeping* eye.
  *Like alliteration, assonance also repeats sound. But the sound
  is in the middle or end of words, rather than the beginning.*

STRUCTURE

For the parts of sentences doing the same work—signaled by the conjunctions *and, or, but*—repeating the grammatical structures adds balance and often picks up rather than smothers the cadence. You've already seen this in many of the foregoing sections. Here, I extend it to something more than a word.

Just to be hired, he may have to take *a drug test, a lie-detector test* (though this is now limited to certain fields), and *a psychological test.*
  Article (a), *adjective* (drug, lie-detector, psychological), *noun*
  (test)—*with all three repeated, the list is more memorable
  than anything varied structures or varied words would evoke.*

There is *the same* delight in the great game of espionage, *the same* malevolent eye for human weakness, *the same* creeping sense of despair at finding oneself on the wrong side of history.

It is everywhere, *it is* cheap, and *it is,* above all, open.

White pine *is too soft,* he reasons, maple *is too sleek,* oak *is too ordinary.*

5

CREDIBLE QUOTATIONS

QUOTATION offers tremendous relief from exposition. It is also far more engaging, perhaps explaining why we'll attend to the speech-laden prose of a novel far longer than a piece of expository writing.

DIRECT

Notice how frequently the *Wall Street Journal* brings people into its stories with a quotation and the effect on the credibility of argument. Suddenly, it's no longer up to the writer to persuade. It's up to the chosen authority.

It's no surprise that Warhol did the guest-star stunt (Halston once observed that Warhol "would go to the opening of a drawer").

"If you see a banker jump out the window, jump after him — there's sure to be profit in it," said Voltaire.

"Trusting the government with your privacy," snorted *Wired* magazine, "is like having a Peeping Tom install your window blinds."

"In the Information Age," says education consultant Margaret Reil, "factual knowledge is plentiful. What is scarce is the intellectual work of giving value to information, of transforming information into useful knowledge systems. This is the work of communities."

INDIRECT

Indirect quotations do not guarantee exact wording, but they still command the authority quoted. Such constructions as *says that*, without quotation marks, indicate the looseness of a quotation.

Irving Clayton, a Canadian poet, observed that his countrymen are right to consider America hell; but only because Canada itself is limbo.

James Harbour, an American productivity expert, argues that by finding ways of stripping out costs without affecting quality or reliability, the Japanese could reduce costs by 40–50%.

The first shot was lobbed back in 1989, when Rushdie, four months into his Ayatollah-decreed death sentence, wrote an eviscerating review of le Carré's thriller "The Russia House"; le Carré responded *by declaring that* Rushdie had brought the "fatwa" upon himself and *criticized* him for going ahead with the paperback edition of "The Satanic Verses," suggesting that

Rushdie put a higher value on cash than on the lives of his publisher's employees.

She once told an interviewer that her Olive Oyl voice was an attempt to imitate the actress ZaSu Pitts.

OPENING WITH A QUOTATION

Opening an entire piece with a quotation sets the tone for all that follows.

"It is my duty," wrote the correspondent for The Times of London at the liberation of the Nazi death camp at Belsen, *"to describe something beyond the imagination of mankind."* That was how I felt in the summer of 1979 when I arrived in Cambodia.

"The source of my painting is the unconscious," Pollock declared, and there was no Abstract Expressionist of whom this was more clearly true.

"I think it of great importance," wrote Gouverneur Morris to George Washington in 1790, advising him on how to furnish the presidential mansion, *"to fix the taste of our country properly . . . everything about you should be substantially good and majestically plain, made to endure."*

"I still have all my arms and legs and I still have my smarts," says Gloria Mason, a 73-year-old widow from Wheaton. *"Where do I go?"* Every morning, millions of men and women—smart, curious, vibrant—face a day with no deadlines, no demands, no schedule.

SHOWING OMISSION

Ellipses (three dots) replace words you are not quoting—when the quotation is too lengthy or when your point is less apparent with the intervening words included.

> The hottest investment in Japan may well be . . . real estate.
> *An ellipsis can also cause a dramatic pause in an ordinary*
> *sentence—much like the interruptive dash (which I prefer).*

"Our requests elicited recurrent clichés and stereotypes: Americans are given to confession. . . . Americans are puritanical. . . . Americans are obsessed with work."

The marriage between Jane and John Clemens was "courteous, considerate and always respectful, and even deferential," their son Sam remembered; "they were always kind toward each other, but . . . there was nothing warmer."

At least six members of the jury cried as Ryan spoke of individual victims, dramatically concluding each description by saying "the defendant killed many wives. . . . The defendant killed many children. . . . The defendant killed many grandparents."

6

CONVERSATIONAL INJECTIONS

LIKE quotations, conversational injections bring the personal into what would otherwise be impersonal and formal. They range from the wry comments to the questions and contractions that populate speech.

COMMENTS

Some words and phrases, slipped in at various points in a sentence, can reveal more of your view than mere declaration, drawing you closer to your reader.

For all their supposed mastery at putting together other peoples' businesses, investment bankers seem lousy at merging their own.

That sounds dandy, but last year was a strong one for the Canadian economy; and these high figures follow several years of low or even negative returns.

Son of one Revolutionary War hero and son-in-law of another, Allan Melvill had, *as we would say today,* good connections.

The system involves the feds in every decision to hire, which is a troubling precedent; and *of course it will make mistakes.*

QUESTIONS

Questions address readers the way imperatives do, engaging their attention. They can also add wry twists to an otherwise sober discussion. But don't sprinkle them indiscriminately—for no effect—as some journalists do. They work best at the beginning of a paragraph, creating bonds with paragraphs that precede or follow.

Could Canada really be near to breaking up after all?
Compare this with Canada could be near to breaking up, but then again it might not be.

Next: women linebackers in the National Football League?

To ensure that shareholders' assets are used wisely, it surely makes sense to pay their stewards handsomely. *But how much is that?*

QUESTIONS ANSWERED

Many writers open a paragraph with a question and keep the reader musing about possible answers through to the end. Fine, if that's the desired effect. More potent, however, is the immediate answer, especially with a fragment.

Does all this seem overdone? Well, yes.
Compare this with the common All this seems overdone.

But which countries should represent these regions. India? Pakistan says no. Brazil? Argentina says no. Nigeria? Everybody says no.

So how much can a novelist get away with? It entirely depends upon whether or not he can sustain our interest by sheer force of persuasive imaginative skill.

. . . Japan's financial system has not always been dominated by banks. Before the second world war, stock and bond markets were thriving. In the early 1930s, half of companies' capital came from issuing shares. Were these markets killed by accident or design?
   Probably a bit of both. . . .

PARENTHETICAL ASIDES

Asides plug in material not directly related to the main idea. Parentheticals can also make it easier for readers to make the leap from subject and predicate or to navigate the elements of a series.

Cheering supporters waved little Union Jacks *(provided by Blair's ever assiduous campaign staff)* and shouted "Tony! Tony!"
   What moves this comment about Blair's staff to an aside? Parentheses. Mere commas would have signaled the reader that the parenthetical material was simply adding a bit of dispensable detail.

Sterling's sci-fi protagonist goes through an implausible procedure *(albeit one based on an extrapolation of some real med-*

ical research) that restores her youth; who would not give most of their worldly goods for that?

She also deserves commendation for teaching *(for better or for worse)* the male publishing establishment a thing or two about how to sell a book.

After all, action movies, with minimal subtitles, cross linguistic barriers more easily than dramas built on dialogue and nuance. *(Boys with toys travel well, the saying goes.)*
    Sometimes an entire sentence is a parenthetical aside.

SLIPPED-IN MODIFIERS (OFTEN AS ASIDES)

Some writers put a modifier in parentheses to inject their opinion or offhandedly highlight something about what's being modified.

Two scraggly fifteen-foot palm trees in white trashcan planters have been brought in for the occasion with the *(unsuccessful)* idea of a festive touch.
    Consider this without the parentheses or without unsuccessful. *The* idea of a festive touch *suddenly becomes* the UNSUCCESSFUL idea, *with the aside far noisier than a mere modifier.*

Durkheim offered an even more specific *(and more dynamic)* and less crystallized concept that is also a nonmaterial social fact—social currents.

Naturally, the anti-smoking ideology presumes *(wrongly)* that both conditions are true.

Like Chelsea [Clinton], they actually seem to like their dysfunctional parents. Unlike her, they don't know *(or care)* much about politics, and their main civic passions are local: jobs, families, and community.

CONTRACTIONS

It used to be that contractions were all but forbidden in formal writing. Then, in the mid-1980s, they began to appear in the news—and since, more broadly. Conversational, they imbue sentences with an (often needed) air of informality.

> *He's* just another yuppie on a power trip.
> *Some editors would still turn this back to* He is.

Given this climate, *it's* hardly surprising that Satan should have metamorphosed from a pitchfork-wielding fiend into the Armani-clad guy next door.

C'mon fellas—time to go all the way.

It was the best forensic advice *I'd* ever seen a candidate get, and Gore had made the most of it: *he'd* soared that night, skewering his opponents on defense policy.

7

STARK ATTACHMENTS

STARK attachments do more to distinguish the professional from the common than any other edit. And all they take is a change in position and the cutting of two or three words.

LEADING PARTS

Most writers merrily run from one independent clause to the next, either joining them in one sentence or letting them stand apart as two. Doing this, they miss the opportunity to link two ideas more closely and build a more compelling structure—one with a touch of suspense. Most leading parts could appear after the subject—less suspenseful, less emphatic.

> *Esteemed in the West as the statesman who ended the cold war,* Mr. Gorbachev is extremely unpopular in Russia, where he is blamed for allowing the Soviet Union to fall apart and for not having pushed reform of the command economy far enough.
> *Shortening what would otherwise have been an independent clause (Mr. Gorbachev is esteemed . . .) and abruptly at-*

taching the phrase to the front of a sentence is a standard edit that too few writers avail themselves of.

Struck by an annual outbreak of filial sentiment, Americans make more long-distance calls on Mother's Day than on any other day of the year.

Neither quite this nor altogether that, terrifically itself yet perpetually ambiguous, Turkey stands alone among the nations.

Like many amateur memoirs, this book may be best appreciated by the writer, not the reader.
A special class of the common embellishment, with a prepositional phrase, this one is attached to the subject that immediately follows. The example here could have been the common This book is like many amateur memoirs and may best. . . .

INNER PARTS

Many writers habitually open their subordinate clauses with *which is, that is, who is.* Taking out the pronoun and verb is a standard edit (in the spirit of Strunk and White's "which hunting") and is one of the easiest you can make to begin building sentences that are less ordinary.

The PC Forum, *an annual conference that attracts some of the biggest names in the computer industry,* is a hard place to get noticed, especially if you are a relatively obscure economist.
The highlighted phrase could have been a dependent clause, which is an annual conference. *Removing the* which is *shortens the sentence and picks up the cadence by adding the elaboration abruptly.*

Last year General Electric, *an American conglomerate,* earned $6.6 billion in after-tax profits by selling everything from fridges to aircraft engines.

Most writers unnecessarily introduce examples with *such as, for example, that is,* and the shorthand *i.e.* and *e.g.* Dropping those openings and replacing the surrounding commas with a pair of dashes provide variety—and pick up the cadence of your sentences.

Then along comes some external force—*a volcano, an asteroid, an ice age*—that changes all the niches and launches a mad scramble for survival.
   An ounce of example is worth a ton of abstraction.

Impressionism's essential project—*the capture of momentary effects of light*—was too insubstantial to fully engage him.

TRAILING PARTS

As with leading and inner parts, what otherwise would be an independent clause can be starkly attached as a trailing part.

The deep intrusive past was never far away—*echoed in a ruin, a habit, a village, a sight not meant to be a reminder but there all the same.*

[My house] is unadorned and functional, inexpressive and solid: it has proved this during the last war, when it went through the bombings, *escaping with some slight damage to the window frames and a few scratches which it still bears with the pride that a veteran bears the scars left by his wounds.*

And as with some other inner parts, you can remove the *who is* or *which is* from a dependent clause and attach the remaining phrase at the end with a dash or comma.

Yet, staying at home can be the most brazen act of all. Or so we learned from Johannes Vermeer—*art's first great homebody.*
This might have been much flatter as Johannes Vermeer— who was art's first great homebody.

Hoping to jazz up vegetables' boring image, the Vegetarian Society, a British group, recently released "Hot Dinner," *an erotic public-service cinema ad bursting with rapid-fire shots of sizzling chilies and oozing peaches.*

8

DEFT CONNECTIONS

MUCH of writing is connecting words and phrases that are doing the same work—multiple subjects, verbs, modifiers, objects. And most writers connect them with conjunctions and commas in common ways. Here are some uncommon connections.

SERIES FROM SHORT TO LONG

Compound subjects and predicates and the elements of pairs or series usually appear as they come out of the writer's mind—haphazardly. Rearranging those elements from short to long and from simple to compound makes them easier for your reader to understand. Start by counting the syllables of each word—and the words of each phrase—and try arranging them from short to long. If there is another way to order the list (such as chronology or increasing importance), short to long may not apply.

> They're *smart, ambitious,* and *uncomplaining.*
> *Compare this with the less orderly* ambitious, smart, and un-complaining—*and with* uncomplaining, ambitious, and smart, *inverted for an emphatic, monosyllabic finish (which would be even more emphatic without the* and).

Bill Gates and his empire command *fear, respect and curiosity* in the world he helped create.

When we say *cliché, stereotype, trite pseudoelegant phrase,* and so on, we imply, among other things, that when used the first time in literature the phrase was original and had a vivid meaning.

That the cancer doctor's three main tools—*surgery, radiation and chemotherapy*—are often of so little use is no surprise: a disease caused by genetic instability requires a genetic remedy.

SERIES WITH AN EXTRA CONJUNCTION

Adding an extra conjunction to a series (usually another *and*) sets each member of the list apart and suggests that all possible members have been included—A and B and C. It can also distinguish pairings in a series—A and B, C and D, and E.

It will take shape, as all civilizations take shape, by the living of it, by work and effort, by trial and error, by *enterprise and adventure and experience.*
   The common form would have been and by enterprise, adventure, and experience. *The extra* and *in the subseries, pulled from the front of the last part of the full series, gets rid of two commas and finishes with a melodic cascade.*

He can *gush and despise, revel and sneer,* as through a bifocal lens.

All through the summer there had been *rumors and waiting and hope against hope,* as there is before wars break out.

Marketing and consumer-products firms like to know who buys what—*and where and when and how.*

SERIES WITHOUT A CONJUNCTION

Dropping a conjunction has the opposite effect of adding a conjunction: creating a series that is not exhaustive, but a mere sampling of possibilities. It also makes your reader see the parts of the series as more separate than joined.

> This 20th century is *baffling, difficult, paradoxical, revolutionary.*
> *When the series ends a sentence, the final word resonates more without the* and.

> *Tattoo parlours, pawnbrokers, discounters* remain.

> It is not merely gems that De Beers is selling, but *symbols, myths, magic.*

> She spent all her time after school inside the houses of kids whose parents were *sometimes farmhands, sometimes mechanics, sometimes unemployed.*

PAIRED CONJUNCTIONS

Paired conjunctions suggest parts of equal importance and require that those parts be of the same (or at least similar) construction. They often connote something remarkable about the pairing. Common pairs: *both . . . and; not only . . . but also; either . . . or, neither . . . nor, just as . . . so.*

> But *just as* software has transformed the Internet, *so* the Internet will transform software.
> *The inversion of* software *and* Internet *to* Internet *and* software, *with a shift in tense from* has transformed *to* will transform, *is signaled by the pair* just as *and* so.

Nothing, *neither* a belief *nor* a piece of stone *nor* a memory, was wasted there, and never has been.

Today, with the globalization of American culture, it's clear that we won *not only* the cold war *but also* the battle for the world's leisure time.

Just as old does not necessarily mean feeble, *(so)* older does not necessarily mean sicker.
> *With* just as . . . so, *you can drop the word* so *if the sentence makes sense without it.*

This was a deal made *both* easier, *and* worse, by the fact that, at the eleventh hour, plummeting deficit estimates from the Congressional Budget Office gave the negotiators an extra $225 billion in projected revenues over five years to play with.

America's navy and air force tend to see a battleship as a big open space containing *either* friends, to be protected, *or* foes, to be destroyed.

STARTING WITH A CONJUNCTION

An obvious way to break a long sentence or two or three independent clauses is to make each clause a sentence. Not so obvious is keeping the conjunction at the start of the next sentence (or two). This has the added advantage of preserving the link between them. True, some of you will be aghast at such flouting of the dictates of your seventh-grade teacher. But what was common two hundred years ago (see Adam Smith's *Wealth of Nations*) is again in vogue (see *The Economist*).

I fear my memories, of which, good and bad, I have far too many. *But* lost friends are better honored with smiles than with tears. *And* having too many memories is better than having too few.

As a single sentence, this could have been a blur. Instead, the periods do their work of separating the three clauses, making them easier to grasp. And the opening conjunctions do their work of linking the three clauses.

Many people choose not to know. *But* what happens when your entire genetic closet is flung open during a routine physical?

The bosses of the world's biggest firms have great freedom to run them as they see fit, and it is almost impossible to compare their decisions to alternatives that were not—and never will be—taken. *Nor* is it easy to separate their personal contributions from plain luck.

You may open a sentence with Nor *when it follows a sentence with a negative verb phrase (generally with the word* not *in it)* . . .

A situation in a book is intensely felt because it reminds us of something that happened to us or to someone we know or knew. *Or,* again, a reader treasures a book mainly because it evokes a country, a landscape, a mode of living which he nostalgically recalls as part of his own past. *Or,* and this is the worst thing a reader can do, he identifies himself with a character in the book.

. . . or with the equivalent, as with will be unable, *which is the same as* will not be able.

SEMICOLONS

Semicolons join independent clauses without using a conjunction, binding two or more closely related ideas that are ideally parallel in construction. They cause a pause longer than a comma, shorter than a period. Some writers use them to link closely related clauses in a paragraph, to distinguish them from looser clauses and ideas.

> The benefits to Africa are obvious; the benefits to America are also obvious.
> *A semicolon at its best, slamming together two parallel ideas and constructions.*

> Breeding racehorses along these lines is sensible; breeding rulers, to the modern mind, is not.

> Brazilians first contemplated a new, inland capital in 1789; the name Brasilia was first suggested in 1822; yet construction did not start until 1956.

> The emblems of American mass culture have infiltrated the remotest outposts: the Coca-Cola logo is on street corners from Kazakhstan to Bora-Bora; CNN emanates from television sets in more than 200 countries; there are more 7-Eleven stores in Japan than in the United States.

COLON LINKING AN EXAMPLE

Like the semicolon, the colon joins in one sentence ideas that might be treated in separate sentences, strengthening the bond between these ideas. This works well for examples.

> Other little things are being changed: Japanese car makers used to paint the parts which most drivers never saw, such as the fuel tank or the drive shafts.

Then, in 1981, IBM introduced the personal computer, causing a market explosion from which emerged some of today's strongest companies: Intel, Microsoft, Compaq.

When you call your bank, you're likely to face a similar stinginess of options, but with luck they'll fit your needs: your account balance, say, or determining whether a deposit has cleared.

Soon hundreds of people were skating in concentric rings around the speakers every weekend afternoon: teen-agers in spandex, 60-year-olds in hiking shorts, Wall Street traders, Broadway dancers, Brooklyn detectives, German bankers, Brazilian nurses, Nigerian vendors, celebrities like Morgan Freeman and Margaux Hemingway bopping along next to bicycle messengers.

COLON LINKING AN ELABORATION

Colons also link elaborations, embellishments, definitions.

New platforms are often troubled early on by a nasty chicken-and-egg problem: consumers will not buy them until lots of compatible products are available, and companies will not develop compatible products until they see a market.
Here, the writer defines the nasty chicken-and-egg problem, *making certain with a colon that you read what follows as the definition.*

But Big Brother is doing his bit: in the struggle against crime, terrorism, deadbeat parents, illegal immigrants and even traffic jams, the government keeps an ever-closer eye on more and more of its citizens.

As a result, American art tells the American story: Americans, like any other people, inscribe their histories, beliefs, attitudes, desires, and dreams in the images they make.

He had imparted the city's traditional philosophy toward visitors: show them no mercy.

PARALLEL CONSTRUCTIONS

Parallel structures intensify the bond between two of a sentence's joined parts and make the sentence easier to read. Any conjunction is a red flag for attending to parallel structure.

Although few realize it, Americans are generally able *to see the files kept on them, to correct mistakes, to block disclosure (sometimes, at least)* and *to learn where information has gone.*

The state, on this view, was best held to certain core functions—*providing public goods such as defense, ensuring the security of persons and property, educating citizenry, and enforcing contracts*—deemed essential for the market to flourish.

For Joyce, a Yuletide tale *"should have food in it, should have snow in it, and it should have gatherings of people, relatives that you don't like, relatives that you do like, and people that you otherwise would never have met."*

We must see and hear things, we must visualize the clothes, the rooms, the manners of an author's people.

THE VERB-FREE ELEMENT

With parallel independent clauses, you can often drop the verb from the second, leaving the reader to insert it mentally, whether singular or plural.

> Her novels *registered* these events most secretly, her letters not at all.
>> *The flatter version of this might have been* and her letters registered these events not at all. *Dropping* and *and* registered these events *shortens the sentence and picks up the cadence.*

> Premises *were* cramped, working capital scarce, infrastructure fragile and the bureaucracy tiresome.

> The trip *is* now a commodity; the tourist, a consumer; the world, a supermarket of travel opportunities trying mightily to satisfy every imaginable taste, temperament, and interest.

> She *supplied* the facts and statistics, I the philosophy and rhetoric, and, together, we have made arguments that stood unshaken through the storms of long years; arguments that no one has answered.

9

ONE-SYLLABLE OPENINGS

SENTENCES obviously get off to a faster start with a one-syllable opening than with words of two or more syllables. And successions of one-syllable openings can (occasionally) bind a paragraph more tightly. Rely on your ear—and restraint—to use these openings for best effect. For they swiftly descend into the common.

IT

Starting a sentence with *It* is generally to be avoided, as in *It is Johnson who damaged . . .* , *It can now be stated with certainty that . . .* , or *It goes without saying that . . .* (why say it?). The reason: something deserving emphasis at the start of a sentence becomes submerged by the fatty opening. But an opening *it* can get a paragraph or entire piece off to a fast, emphatic, monosyllabic start.

It is with noble sentiments that bad literature gets written.
   Notice how clean this opening is.

It is not at all hard to see how the American economy could support a much larger medical sector; it is, however, very hard to see how the U.S. Government will manage to pay for its share of that sector's costs.

It is wartime; no new labor is coming in from the old countries across the seas.

It is that old, old issue with those old, old battered labels—the issue of Isolationism versus Internationalism.

THERE

Opening with *There is* or *There are* is one of the most natural ways of starting a sentence in speech and thus in print. So natural that it tires from overuse. So, much like the opening *It*, the opening *There* is something generally to avoid. Reserve it for the special needs of conversational punch and variety.

> *There* is little artistic relevance in classifying rap music, a definite and unique rap form, as poetry.
> *Starting with* There *gives this sentence an easy, natural flow.*
> *The alternative*—Classifying rap music, a definite and unique rap form, as poetry has little artistic relevance—*is bumpier.*

There were many stories of courage that night.

There may have been another factor: Fuchs was complaining.

There has been no post-revolutionary toppling of statues and icons.

THIS

As a pronoun for something that has just been mentioned or is about to be, *This* is one of those useful monosyllables for opening a sentence. And as a pronoun, it's essential.

This is a good day to take a close look at a famous speech. *This forward reference is a common opening sentence for expository writing of all types.* This *refers to what follows: a* good day. *(The same goes for its plural,* these.*)*

This would be wizardry indeed.

This is quite a declaration.

This contradiction necessitates that we speak of money euphemistically or keep quiet.

THAT

As a pronoun for something just mentioned, *That* is another of those useful monosyllables. But as with the backward reference for *This,* be sure that it is perfectly clear what *That* refers to.

That is why the best outcome from Kyoto would have been a modest, politically workable agreement to curb emissions of greenhouse gases pending further study. *A pronoun doing its duty: standing for many more words preceding it.*

That will teach them to disrespect their bodies.

That leaves Mr. Mbeki treading a delicate line between keeping them happy and suffocating the businesses on which he knows full well economic success depends.

That, in fact, is part of the problem: the golfer has all the time in the world to think.

WHAT

The structure of this can get confusing, depending on whether *What* is a pronoun or adjective.

> *What* a shock it must be for Koreans to discover that what they thought was a rich, rapidly growing homeland with near-perfect job security is in fact teetering on the edge of bankruptcy.
> *Adjective modifying* shock.

What they didn't know proved liberating.

What we hear is not necessarily what is said.

What made Max Beerbohm's malice merry was its distant, generally impersonal, and always playful quality.

EXEMPLARY SENTENCES

Clive Crook

"E U R O P E ' S   G A M B L E "

Repetition of M sound

Colon linking an example

Highlight

Opening embellishment

Closing clause comments

Highlight

Dashed inner part

IN May 1998, Europe's governments will make the most momentous decision about Europe's future since the creation of the Common Market in 1958: they will say which countries will be founder members of the new monetary union. Recently they underlined their determination to stick to the timetable laid down in the Maastricht treaty. The meeting next May will decide not only which countries are to go forward in the first wave but also the parties to be fixed "irrevocably" from January 1st, 1999, when EMU comes into force.

——Only a few months ago, the monetary union project seemed to be faltering, to the relief of Britain's Labour government, among others, who would rather the subject went away for a few years. Now it is back on schedule, its momentum renewed. At last the fact is sinking in: EMU is coming—a "wide" EMU, including Italy, Spain and Portugal—

and it is coming whether Europe's voters like it or not.

Opening embellishment

On the whole, and to the extent that they have a view one way or the other, they seem not to like it. This should count for some-

Opening "this"

Direct address

thing, you might think, given that the EU's 15 countries are democracies.

Complicated clause

But Europe's politicians appear to think otherwise: so far they have made next to no

Colon linking an elaboration.

effort to educate their electorates on the benefits and drawbacks of what is proposed. Why? Because this is not (or not yet) an issue

Parenthetical aside

that divides people neatly along party-political lines. It cuts across those lines—and

Opening conjunction

no politician in Europe needs reminding of what happened to Britain's Tories when they put their disagreement on this subject frankly before the public. As a result, the lack of po-

Repetition of P sound

litical preparation for the EMU is almost total. This is matched by an equally comprehensive lack of economic preparation.

Question answered with fragment

Does this matter? Yes. Because of it, the benefits of monetary union will be smaller than they might have been and the drawbacks bigger, possibly catastrophic. A project that makes good sense in principle has become far, far riskier than it ever need have

Opening "It"

been. Why run this danger? It cannot be

Direct address

right, you might think, to say that there has

Conditioned clause

been no preparation for EMU: only consider

Colon linking an elaboration

Repetition of "preparation"

the time and effort that Europe's governments have devoted to the Maastricht "convergence criteria." True, plenty of time and effort have been spent—but to very little use-

Interruptive dash

ful effect.

The trouble with the Maastricht criteria is

not mainly that they have been fiddled (though they have been outlandishly and will be even more so before next May) but that they were beside the point in the first place. The treaty called for four main kinds of con- vergence: on inflation, interest rates, budget deficits and public debt.

Colon linking an elaboration

Multiplied verb, Multiplied adjectives

These rules were, and remain, a mixture of the unnecessary, the irrelevant and the counter-productive. But what matters far more are two convergence criteria that the treaty does not mention at all: labour-market flexibility and national responses to changes in interest rates. When EMU comes into operation, governments will no longer be able to use changes in monetary policy to stabilize their national economies—cutting interest rates and depreciating their currencies in recessions, raising rates and appreciating their currencies in booms.

Opening conjunction

Colon linking an elaboration

Interruptive dash

Parallel construction

Short form to start a paragraph

—This is a big loss. In Europe at present monetary policy shoulders the larger part of the burden of adjustment to economic fluctuations. Once national monetary policy is abolished for this purpose, the burden must fall elsewhere: partly on fiscal policy and partly on the labour market. Bizarrely, Europe's governments say they will not rely much on fiscal policy. (Germany's proposed "stability pact", which makes the Maastricht budget-deficit criterion a permanent rule, seeks to formalise this self-denying, self-destructive ordinance.) So Europe's nations will be left with only changes in wages to adjust to swings of the economic cycle. Therefore, if France, say, should suffer an

Opening "this"

Opening embellishment

Repetition of "partly"

Colon linking an elaboration

Parenthetical aside

Repetition of D sound

economic downturn once EMU is up and running, the only remedy for unemployment will be lower wages.

In flexible, deregulated labour markets (such as America's), a small reduction in wages is enough to spur employment powerfully; in rigid, highly regulated ones, bigger pay-cuts are required. Europe's labour markets are the most rigid in the world. Unemployment rises more in Europe than in America during economic downturns. Putting this right is essential if the political and economic risks of EMU are to be minimized. But governments are doing almost nothing and initiatives such as the "social chapter" threaten to make the problem worse. The other missing convergence criterion is responsiveness to interest rates. When Europe's new central bank puts interest rates up in order to reduce inflationary pressures across the EU, the precise effect will depend on the fine structure of national financial systems. For instance, the effect will be smaller in countries where housing finance is arranged mainly on a fixed-rate basis rather than on a variable-rate basis. In this way and others, when the central bank changes its interest rate the effect will differ in strength from country to country: a change sufficient to modern demand in one country may be enough to induce a recession in another. Sensible governments planning for EMU would have addressed this by now.

The lack of inquiry and debate about EMU in Europe has been lamentable. Britain has had a debate, of sorts—but not

Margin annotations:

Opening embellishment

Semicolon links parallel clauses

Common direct form

Common direct form

Opening conjunction

Highlight

Repetition of "convergence criterion"

Opening embellishment

Parallel construction

Colon linking an example

Common conditioned form

Common direct form

Repetition of L sound

Interruptive dash

an illuminating one. The Tories divide into warring camps, one for EMU and the other against, neither side caring in the least about details or circumstances. Elsewhere there has been hardly any debate at all. Yet whether EMU is a success or a failure turns entirely on the details and the circumstances. Far too little is being done to make it the success it could be or to minimize the dangers. When you consider how steep the costs of failure might be—not merely a needlessly deep recession nor even the collapse of an ill-constructed monetary union but the coming apart of the EU itself—these omissions are nothing short of outrageous. And 1998 will show them to be so.

Margin annotations:

Common direct form

Short form to start a point

Dashed inner part

Short form to finish paragraph

Repetition of "details and circumstances"

Repetition of ee sounds and "ssion" sounds

Opening conjunction

Permission to reprint
granted by *The Economist*

"MASTER OF HIS DOMAIN"

THE funniest man in America isn't on television. He doesn't do stand-up or talk shows or American Express ads. He doesn't make silly faces or rude noises. He doesn't try to spin his own indiscretions into pretentious art. His jokes aren't about "nothing"; they're not even about himself. Indeed, his specialty is making black comedy out of such unfunny objects as high finance and gutter journalism, Hollywood tunnel vision and Washington doublespeak, human vanity and greed.

— Over a five-decade career, Larry Gelbart, 72, has wielded his virtuoso comedy skills in radio, TV, film and theater and worked with everyone from Bob Hope and Sid Caesar to John Belushi and Bill Murray. Along the way, he has proven himself a master of virtually every comedic form, but whether it's a vaudeville takeoff on Plautus ("A Funny Thing Happened on the Way to the Forum"), gender-bending farce ("Tootsie"), political

Margin annotations: Parallel construction · Highlight · Opening embellishment · Contractions · Semicolon contractions · Parallel pairs · Added conjunction · Parallel pairs · Parenthetical asides

satire ("Mastergate") or half-hour television ("M*A*S*H"), two constants can be found: a consummate craftsman's love of language and a disappointed idealist's rage at a corrupt, tawdry, sanctimonious and hypocritical world. Those same two qualities animate Gelbart's new book of essays, "Laughing Matters" (due next month from Random House), and they also percolate throughout his conversation, along with lots of puns, aphorisms and jokes.

The man is not only a compulsive writer— he's currently working on a musical stage version of "A Star is Born," a film version of "Chicago," a remake of the Peter Cook–Dudley Moore comedy "Bedazzled" and an HBO series about a Beverly Hills plastic surgeon—but he's also a reflexive ad-libber, a hyperkinetic talker who says it would be nice to have "a dimmer" in his brain. In his later work, Gelbart has skewered the tabloid wars ("Weapons of Mass Distraction"), corporate takeovers ("Barbarians at the Gate") and Hollywood venality ("City of Angels"), and when he talks about comedy writing, it quickly becomes clear that he is equally indignant about the state of his own art. As Gelbart sees it, people have become increasingly cynical about politics, increasingly resigned to being ineffectual receivers of bad news. And humor, in turn, has grown increasingly escapist, juvenile and bitchy. In more and more movie comedies, he observes, "with has been replaced by wind," and on television, the serious themes once examined by shows like "All

---

Margin annotations:

- Repetition of C sound
- Series short to long
- Parenthetical aside
- Interruptive dash
- Parallel structure

- Colon links example
- Common multiplied form
- Highlight
- Interruptive dash
- Indirect quotation
- Highlights
- Parenthetical asides
- Repetition
- Opening conjunction
- Direct quotation

Repetition

Direct quotation

Quotation showing omission

Direct quotation

Common multiplied form

Trailing part

Trailing part

Parenthetical asides

Common multiplied form

Conditioned "that" clause

Opening embellishment

in the Family," and "M*A*S*H" have given way to the stupid bedroom and bathroom jokes of shows like "Veronica's Closet." "It's all about did she, will she or won't she," he says. "It's like Doris Day on speed. It's all about doing it and each other's pee-pees." He says he thinks it's great that a show as "hip and offbeat" as "Seinfeld" is a hit but adds that its wackiness "is a studied wacky—they're like professional kooks." He calls "Def Comedy Jam" "a miracle of bad taste . . . riot comedy, not a comedy riot," and says of "Friends," "It's just attitude, and 'tude is easier to write than jokes." Gelbart does give high marks to "The X-Files" ("The funniest guy on TV is David Duchovny—he's always saying things that are very flippant in situations that are anything but that"), C-Span ("I like aliens of any sort") and "Politically Incorrect" ("It reminds me of the old days, when people were more outspoken"). Certainly comedy writing has changed considerably since Gelbart began working back in the 40's and 50's. Among the developments that Gelbart says have changed his craft are a global film market that discounts verbal comedy and the comedy of ideas, an audience that has lost "the ability to be ashamed," and shorter attention spans that make the sort of story-based humor once practiced by comics like Danny Thomas harder to sustain. At the same time, he believes, audiences' standards have slipped: forget finely crafted jokes and sophisticated wordplay—these days, an embarrassing revelation or a few dirty words are enough to get a reaction. "You really had to earn the laughter in the old days," Gelbart says. "Now we've got shock in place of wit, shock even in place of jokes. And some people aren't even shocked: they're just laughing because, 'Hey, this guy talks just like me.' "

—In addition, Gelbart argues, TV writing has grown more solipsistic: whereas television once attracted people trained in radio, film and theater, it's now the province of lifelong couch potatoes with a fondness for inside jokes. And on sitcoms, those jokes are increasingly crafted by committees. "There's a custom out here now called table writing," he says. "A draft will be prepared by one or two writers, and the staff will sit around a table and try to get in as many new lines as possible. It is not an art being practiced here. It is a product being manufactured to as rigid a set of standards as getting all the right ingredients inside a bottle of Coca-Cola." Although such sharply held views about Hollywood and big business have fueled some of Gelbart's most recent and savage work, he says it's becoming harder to write satire when reality itself feels so surreal.

— In a time when the President's sex life is front-page news and disgraced ambassadors are being exhumed at Arlington, he says, the most one can do is "stay about five seconds ahead of the curve." "A large part of you doesn't want to be funny about it at all," he adds. "A large part of you wants to cry. Sure, my stuff has gotten darker in recent years, but life's gotten darker. As one gets ready for the final curtain, the process enables you to stop

Margin annotations:
- Direct quotation
- Repetition of "shock"
- Exclamation
- Opening embellishment
- Colon linking an example
- Opening conjunction
- Direct quotation
- Parallel structure
- Passive voice
- Indirect quotation
- Opening embellishment
- Parallel structure

denying as much as you have about where
you're going and what's around you while
you're still here. And even if that weren't the   Opening
process, you have to admit, these are pretty   conjunction
scandalous times. I think reporters have be-
come the new satirists."

Permission to reprint granted
by the *New York Times*

SOURCES

1. COMMON FORMS

Direct

"Those Magical Mushrooms," *The Economist* 345, no. 8048 (20 December 1997): 93.

Bob Morris, "Let Them Eat Elsewhere," *New York Times Magazine*, 19 October 1997, sec. 6, p. 91.

Floyd Norris, "Korean Crisis: Blame the Lenders," *New York Times*, 14 December 1997, sec. 3, p. 1.

"Poetic Injustice," *The Economist* 345, no. 8048 (20 December 1997): 129.

Embellished

Alabama Isn't So Different," *The Economist* 345, no. 8039 (18 October 1997): 27.

Tina Rosenberg, "To Hell and Back," *New York Times Magazine*, 28 December 1997, sec. 6, p. 32.

"Ambiguity's Path to Murder," *The Economist* 345, no. 8039 (18 October 1997): 47.

"Why Pagodas Don't Fall Down," *The Economist* 345, no. 8048 (20 December 1997): 121.

Complicated

Judith Shulevitz, "Prematurely Correct," *New York Times Book Review*, 14 December 1997, sec. 7, p. 18.

Isabelle de Courtivron, "Rebel without a Cause," *New York Times Book Review*, 14 December 1997, sec. 7, p. 14.

"Those Magical Mushrooms," *The Economist* 345, no. 8098 (20 December 1997): 95.
"The Birth of a New Species," *The Economist* 339, no. 7967 (25 May 1996): 4.

Conditioned

"Greeting the Dragon," *The Economist* 345, no. 8040 (25 October 1997): 15.
"A Beauty Is Born," *The Economist* 345, no. 8040 (25 October 1997): 94.
"Crash, Dammit," *The Economist* 345, no. 8039 (18 October 1997): 13.
Max Frankel, "A Case of Sheep v. Coyotes," *New York Times Magazine*, 21 December 1997, sec. 6, p. 30.
"Glittering Gadfly," *The Economist* 346, no. 8054 (7 February 1998): 65.
"Watching Where You Eat," *The Economist* 346, no. 8053 (31 January 1998): 87.

Multiplied

Sarah Boxer, "One Casualty of the Women's Movement: Feminism," *New York Times*, 14 December 1997, sec. 4, p. 3.
"Those Magical Mushrooms," *The Economist* 345, no. 8048 (20 December 1997): 93.
Jack Miles, "Religion Makes a Comeback (Belief to Follow)," *New York Times Magazine*, 7 December 1997, sec. 6, p. 56.
Jeffrey Rosen, "The New Look of Liberalism on the Court," *New York Times Magazine*, 5 October 1997, sec. 6, p. 60.

2. OCCASIONAL SHORT FORMS

Fragments

Robert J. Samuelson, "The Attack Culture," *Washington Post*, 12 March 1997, sec. A, p. 19.
Louis Menand, "How Eliot Became Eliot," *New York Review of Books* 54, no. 8 (15 May 1997): 27.
"Back to the Garage," *The Economist* 339, no. 7967 (25 May 1996): 5.
"If Wall Street Falters," *The Economist* 340, no. 7973 (6 July 1996): 119.

To start a paragraph or point

Stanley Kauffmann, *Distinguishing Features* (Baltimore: Johns Hopkins University Press, 1994), p. 10.

"Too Far on Forfeitures," *New York Times*, 26 June 1996, sec. A, p. 18.
"A Surprise in the Woods," *The Economist* 344, no. 8026 (19 July 1997): p. 31.
What's Going On (Washington, D.C.: Benton Foundation, 1997), p. 10.

To finish a paragraph or point

Paul Krugman, "Does Getting Old Cost Society Too Much?" *New York Times Magazine*, 9 March 1997, sec. 6, p. 60.
James Surowiecki, "The Publisher's Curse," *New York Times Magazine*, 31 May 1998, sec. 6, p. 24.
"Time for Reform?" *The Economist* 345, no. 8044 (22 November 1997): 65.
Jeffrey Goldberg, "Our Africa," *New York Times Magazine*, 2 March 1997, sec. 6, p. 35.

Pairs and trios

Vladimir Nabokov, *Lectures on Literature* (1980; New York: Harcourt Brace Jovanovich, 1982), p. 5.
Michael Lewis, *Liar's Poker* (New York: Penguin, 1989), p. 13.
Henry R. Luce, *The American Century* (New York: Farrar and Rinehart, 1941), p. 22.
Cicero, on Julius Caesar.

3. DRAMATIC FLOURISHES

Interruptive dashes

Hubert B. Herring, "Diary," *New York Times*, 18 May 1997, sec. 4, p. 2.
Henry R. Luce, *The American Century* (New York: Farrar and Rinehart, 1941), p. 15.
Paul Berman, "Biker Days," *New Yorker Magazine* 71, no. 22 (31 July 1995): 78.
Michiko Kakutani, "Planet of the Blind: Passing as a Person Who Can See," *New York Times*, 23 December 1997, sec. E, p. 6.

Imperatives

"America the Unmighty," *The Economist* 345, no. 8045 (29 November 1997): 17.
Edwin Dobb, "Where the Good Begins," *Harper's* 297, no. 1778 (July 1998): 60.
"The Tyranny of Success," in *Survey of the Software Industry* (insert), *The Economist* 339, no. 7967 (25 May 1996): 9.

"System Failure," in *International Banking Survey*, *The Economist* 339, no. 7963 (27 April 1996): 6.

Direct address

James K. Glassman, washingtonpost.com, 11 June 1997.
"We Know You're Reading This," *The Economist* 338, no. 7952 (10 February 1996): 27.
Mary Lee Settle, *Turkish Reflections: A Biography of a Place* (1991; New York: Simon & Schuster, 1992), p. xvii.
"The Next Revolution," in *Survey: Business in Eastern Europe*, *The Economist* 345, no. 8044 (22 November 1997): 3.

Recasts

Andrew Sullivan, "When Plagues End," *New York Times Magazine*, 10 November 1996, sec. 6, p. 55.
Jack Miles, "Religion Makes a Comeback. (Belief to Follow)," *New York Times Magazine*, 7 December 1997, sec. 6, p. 58.
Michiko Kakutani, Planet of the Blind: Passing as a Person Who Can See," *New York Times*, 23 December 1997, sec. E, p. 6.
Jack Miles, "Religion Makes a Comeback. (Belief to Follow)," *New York Times Magazine*, 7 December 1997, sec. 6, p. 56.

Reversals

Paul Krugman, "Does Getting Old Cost Society Too Much?" *New York Times Magazine*, 9 March 1997, sec. 6, p. 60.
Henry R. Luce, *The American Century* (New York: Farrar and Rinehart, 1941), p. 7.
Vivian Gornick, "An American Exile in America," *New York Times Magazine*, 2 March 1997, sec. 6, p. 28.
Primo Levi, *Other People's Trades* (London: Michael Joseph, 1989; London: Abacus, 1990), p. 27.

Inversions

"The End of the Miracle?" *The Economist* 345, no. 8047 (13 December 1997): 18.
"Lean Enough?" *The Economist* 338, no. 7952 (10 February 1996): 60.
Kevin Barry, "Still Clueless," *New York Times Book Review*, 7 December 1997, sec. 7, p. 46.

Michiko Kakutani, "To Hell with Him," *New York Times Magazine*, 7 December 1997, sec. 6, p. 38.

Cascades

Mary Lee Settle, *Turkish Reflections: A Biography of a Place* (1991; New York: Simon & Schuster, 1992), p. 35.

Vladimir Nabokov, *Lectures on Literature* (1980; New York: Harcourt Brace Jovanovich, 1982), p. 285.

Elizabeth Marshall Thomas, "Horse Sense," *New York Review of Books* 44, no. 8 (15 May 1997): 11.

Lawrence Weschler, "When Fountainheads Collide," *New Yorker Magazine* 73, no. 38 (8 December 1997): 67.

First and last

"The Birth of a New Species," in *Survey of the Software Industry* (insert), *The Economist* 339, no. 7967 (25 May 1996): 3.

Vladimir Nabokov, *Lectures on Literature* (1980; New York: Harcourt Brace Jovanovich, 1982), p. 3.

Henry R. Luce, *The American Century* (New York: Farrar and Rinehart, 1941), p. 5.

William Safire, "Day of Infamy," *New York Times Magazine*, 7 December 1997, sec. 6, p. 30.

Exclamations

Michael Kinsley, Op-Ed, *Washington Post*, 16 April 1997, sec. A, p. 17.

Henry R. Luce, *The American Century* (New York: Farrar and Rinehart, 1941), p. 34.

David Wallace, "Lost Luggage," *New York Times Magazine*, 21 December 1997, sec. 6, p. 19.

Daniel D'Ambrosio, "Leggo My Logo," *New York Times Magazine*, 5 October 1997, sec. 6, p. 23.

Interjections

Richard Cohen, "The Army's Search and Self-Destroy Mission," *Washington Post*, 5 June 1997, sec. A, p. 21.

"Tough at the Top," *The Economist*, 338, no. 7947 (6 January 1996): 47.

Mary Cantwell, "Still at Work on a Self," *New York Times Magazine*, 9 March 1997, sec. 6, p. 57.

James Baldwin, *Notes of a Native Son* (Boston: Beacon, 1955, 1957, 1983), p. 15.

Highlights

"System Failure," in *International Banking Survey, The Economist* 339, no. 7963 (27 April 1996): 6.
Richard Wright, *12 Million Black Voices* (New York: Viking, 1941), p. 99.
Henry R. Luce, *The American Century* (New York: Farrar and Rinehart, 1941), p. 9.
"Plenty of Gloom," *The Economist* 345, no. 8048 (20 December 1997): 20.

4. ELEGANT REPETITIONS

Word

Vladimir Nabokov, *Lectures on Literature* (1980; New York: Harcourt Brace Jovanovich, 1982), p. 3.
Henry R. Luce, *The American Century* (New York: Farrar and Rinehart, 1941), p. 6.
Henry Han Xi Lau, "I Was a Member of the Kung Fu Crew," *New York Times Magazine*, 19 October 1997, sec. 6, p. 54.
Mary Lee Settle, *Turkish Reflections: A Biography of a Place* (1991; New York: Simon & Schuster, 1992), p. 17.

Root

"Stop the Rot," *The Economist* 350, no. 8102 (16 January 1999): 19.
Primo Levi, *Other People's Trades* (London: Michael Joseph, 1989; London: Abacus, 1990), p. 27.
"The Birth of a New Species," in *Survey of the Software Industry* (insert), *The Economist* 339, no. 7967 (25 May 1996): 3.
Stanley Kauffmann, "sex, lies, and videotape," in *Distinguishing Features* (Baltimore: Johns Hopkins University Press, 1994), p. 133.

Prefix or suffix

Henry R. Luce, *The American Century* (New York: Farrar and Rinehart, 1941), p. 33.
Vladimir Nabokov, *Lectures on Literature* (1980; New York: Harcourt Brace Jovanovich, 1982), p. 372.
Michael Parfit, "Breathless," *New York Times Book Review*, 7 December 1997, sec. 7, p. 24.

Michael Lewis, "Heartless Donors," *New York Times Magazine,* 14 December 1997, sec. 6, p. 46.

Preposition

Richard Wright, *12 Million Black Voices* (New York: Viking, 1941), p. 100.

Henry R. Luce, *The American Century* (New York: Farrar and Rinehart, 1941), p. 15.

Vladimir Nabokov, *Lectures on Literature* (1980; New York: Harcourt Brace Jovanovich, 1982), p. 5.

Elisabeth Bumiller, "The Politics of Personality," *New York Times Magazine,* 2 November 1997, sec. 6, p. 38.

Sound

Merriam-Webster Online Edition of Explorer (m~w.com), 16 December 1997.

"System failure," in *International Banking Survey, The Economist* 339, no. 7963 (27 April 1996): 6.

Michiko Kakutani, "Taking Out the Trash," *New York Times Magazine,* 8 June 1997, sec. 6, p. 34.

William Shakespeare, *Richard II* 1.2.74.

Structure

"We Know You're Reading This," *The Economist* 338, no. 7952 (10 February 1996): 27.

Robert Harris, "I, Spy," *New Yorker Magazine* 73, no. 15 (9 June 1997): 98.

"The Birth of a New Species," in *Survey of the Software Industry* (insert), *The Economist* 339, no. 7967 (25 May 1996): 4.

Witold Rybczynski, "This New House," *New York Review of Books* 44, no. 8 (15 May 1997): 24.

5. CREDIBLE QUOTATIONS

Direct

Michiko Kakutani, "The United States of Andy," *New York Times Magazine,* 17 November 1996, sec. 6, p. 34.

"Coping with the Ups and Downs," in *International Banking Survey, The Economist* 339, no. 7963 (27 April 1996): 3.

"We Know You're Reading This," *The Economist* 338, no. 7947 (10 February 1996): p. 27.

What's Going On (Washington, D.C.: Benton Foundation, 1997), p. 10.

Indirect

"Limbo, Seen from Hell," *The Economist* 339, no. 7964 (4 May 1996): 73.
"Lean Enough?" *The Economist* 338, no. 7952 (10 February 1996): 59.
Vanessa Friedman, "Fax from London," in Talk of the Town, *New Yorker Magazine* 73, no. 38 (8 December 1997): 37.
Rick Lyman, "Mae Questel, 89, behind Betty Boop and Olive Oyl," *New York Times*, 8 January 1998, sec. B, p. 9.

Opening with a quotation

John Pilger, "America's Long Affair with Pol Pot," *Harper's* 297, no. 1778 (July 1998): 15.
Robert Hughes, "American Visions," *Time*, special issue, May 1997, 37.
Ibid.
Roxanne Roberts, "Holiday Park's Senior Class," *Washington Post*, 2 June 1997, sec. D, p. 1.

Showing omission

"Get Real," *The Economist* 342, no. 8009 (22 March 1997): 97.
"How the World Sees Us" (introduction to a special issue of the *New York Times Magazine*), 8 June 1997, sec. 6, p. 37.
Andrew Hoffman, *Inventing Mark Twain: The Lives of Samuel Langhorne Clemens* (New York: Morrow, 1997), p. 3.
Lois Romano, "McVeigh Jurors Sob at Victims' Pain," *Washington Post*, 5 June 1997, sec. A, p. 15.

6. CONVERSATIONAL INJECTIONS

Comments

"Eviction in the City," *The Economist* 342, no. 7964, no. 8007 (8 March 1997): 85.
"Limbo, Seen from Hell," *The Economist* 339, no. 7964 (4 May 1996): 74.
Andrew Delbanco, "The Great Leviathan," *New York Review of Books* 44, no. 8 (15 May 1997): 18.
"We Know You're Reading This," *The Economist* 338, no. 7952 (10 February 1996): 27.

Questions

"Shaking Canada," *The Economist* 337, no. 7937 (21 October 1995): 41.

"A Wealth of Working Women," *The Economist* 339, no. 7969 (8 June 1996): 28.

"The Need for Greed," *The Economist* 339, no. 7964 (4 May 1996): 80.

Questions answered

Robert J. Samuelson, "Telephone Straddle," *Washington Post*, 14 May 1997, sec. A, p. 21.

"To Bury or to Praise," *The Economist* 337, no. 7937 (21 October 1995): 27.

"The Philosopher's Pupil," *The Economist* 334, no. 7897 (14 January 1995): 77.

"A Cautionary Tale," in *Survey: Japanese Finance The Economist* 343, no. 8023 (28 June 1997): 5.

Parenthetical asides

John Cassidy, "Rosy-Digited Dawn," *New Yorker Magazine* 73, no. 11 (12 May 1997): 7.

Paul Krugman, "Does Getting Old Cost Society Too Much?" *New York Times Magazine*, 9 March 1997, sec. 6, p. 60.

Karen Lehrman, "The Original Valley Girl," *New York Times Book Review*, 4 January 1998, sec. 7, p. 27.

Michiko Kakutani, "The Culture Zone," *New York Times Magazine*, 8 June 1997, sec. 6, p. 32.

Slipped-in modifiers (often as asides)

Robert Klitgaard, *Tropical Gangsters* (New York: Basic Books, 1990), p. 2.

George Ritzer, *Sociological Theory*, 4th ed. (New York: McGraw-Hill, 1992), p. 86.

Robert J. Samuelson, "Anti-Smoking Hysteria," *Washington Post*, 23 April 1997, sec. A, p. 21.

Ian Fisher, "The No-Complaints Generation," *New York Times Magazine*, 5 October 1997, sec. 6, p. 68.

Contractions

Michiko Kakutani, "To Hell with Him." *New York Times Magazine*, 7 December 1997, sec. 6, p. 38.

Ibid., p. 37.

William Safire, "Day of Infamy," *New York Times Magazine*, 7 December 1997, sec. 6, p. 32.

Joe Klein, "Learning to Run," *New Yorker Magazine* 73, no. 38 (8 December 1997): 53.

7. STARK ATTACHMENTS

Leading parts

Alessandra Stanley, "From Perestroika to Pizza: Gorbachev Stars in TV Ad," *New York Times*, 3 December 1997, sec. A, p. 1.

"The Death of Distance," in *A Survey of Telecommunications* (insert), *The Economist* 336, no. 7934 (30 September 1995): 5.

Mary Lee Settle, *Turkish Reflections: A Biography of a Place* (1991; New York: Simon & Schuster, 1992), p. ix.

Wendy Kaminer, "Fool for Love," *New York Times Book Review*, 14 December 1997, sec. 7, p. 32.

Inner parts

"The Tyranny of Success," in *Survey of the Software Industry* (insert), *The Economist* 339, no. 7967 (25 May 1996): 9.

"The Need for Greed," *The Economist* 339, no. 7964 (4 May 1996): 80.

"The Birth of a New Species," in *Survey of the Software Industry* (insert), *The Economist* 339, no. 7967 (25 May 1996): 9.

Simon Schama, "Cézanne's Mission," *New Yorker Magazine* 72, no. 16 (17 June 1996): 92.

Trailing parts

Mary Lee Settle, *Turkish Reflections: A Biography of a Place* (1991; New York: Simon & Schuster, 1992), p. 26.

Primo Levi, *Other People's Trades* (London: Michael Joseph, 1989; London: Abacus, 1990), p. 1.

Deborah Solomon, "The Stay at Home Life as Muse," *New York Times*, 20 March 1997, sec. C, p. 1.

David Wallis, "The Joy of Vegetables," *New York Times Magazine*, 12 July 1998, sec. 6, p. 13.

8. DEFT CONNECTIONS

Series from short to long

Ian Fisher, "The No-Complaints Generation," *New York Times Magazine*, 5 October 1997, sec. 6, p. 68.

"The Tyranny of Success," in *Survey of the Software Industry* (insert), *The Economist* 339, no. 7967 (25 May 1996): 9.

Vladimir Nabokov, *Lectures on Literature* (1980); New York: Harcourt Brace Jovanovich, 1982, p. 346.

Nicholas Wade, "Can the Common Cold Cure Cancer?" *New York Times Magazine,* 21 December 1997, sec. 6, p. 34.

Series with an extra conjunction

Henry R. Luce, *The American Century* (New York: Farrar and Rinehart, 1941), p. 34.

Stanley Kauffmann, *Distinguishing Features* (Baltimore: Johns Hopkins University Press, 1994), p. 15.

Mary Lee Settle, *Turkish Reflections: A Biography of a Place* (1991; New York: Simon & Schuster, 1992), p. 29.

"We Know You're Reading This," *The Economist* 338, no. 7947 (10 February 1996): 27.

Series without a conjunction

Henry R. Luce, *The American Century* (New York: Farrar and Rinehart, 1941), p. 29.

"The Mall of Dreams," *The Economist* 339, no. 7964 (4 May 1996): 23.

"Glass with Attitude," *The Economist* 345, no. 8048 (20 December 1997): 113.

Vivian Gornick, "An American Exile in America," *New York Times Magazine,* 2 March 1997, sec. 6, p. 28.

Paired conjunctions

"The Birth of a New Species," in *Survey of the Software Industry* (insert), *The Economist* 339, no. 7967 (25 May 1996): 4.

Mary Lee Settle, *Turkish Reflections: A Biography of a Place* (1991; New York: Simon & Schuster, 1992), p. 16.

Michiko Kakutani, "Taking Out the Trash," *New York Times Magazine,* 8 June 1997, sec. 6, p. 34.

Jack Rosenthal, "The Age Boom," *New York Times Magazine,* 9 March 1997, sec. 6, p. 42.

"The Lovebirds' Budget," *The Economist* 343, no. 8016 (10 May 1997): 16.

"Select Enemy. Delete," *The Economist* 342, no. 8007 (8 March 1997): 24.

Starting with a conjunction

Mary Cantwell, "Still at Work on a Self," *New York Times Magazine,* 9 March 1997, sec. 6, p. 57.

Stephen S. Hall, "Genome Dread," *New York Times Magazine,* 18 January 1998, sec. 6, p. 12.

"The Need for Greed," *The Economist,* 339, no. 7964 (4 May 1996): 80.

Vladimir Nabokov, *Lectures on Literature* (1980; New York: Harcourt Brace Jovanovich, 1982), p. 4.

Semicolons

Jeffrey Goldberg, "Our Africa," *New York Times Magazine,* 2 March 1997, sec. 6, p. 77.

"Monarchs and Mountebanks," *The Economist* 345, no. 8048 (20 December 1997): 62.

"Capital Punishments," *The Economist* 345, no. 8048 (20 December 1997): 69.

Michiko Kakutani, "Taking Out the Trash," *New York Times Magazine,* 8 June 1997, sec. 6, p. 34.

Colon linking an example

"Lean Enough?" *The Economist* 338, no. 795d (10 February 1996): 59.

"The Birth of a New Species," in *Survey of the Software Industry* (insert), *The Economist* 339, no. 7967 (25 May 1996): 3.

Hubert B. Herring, "Diary," *New York Times,* 18 May 1997, sec. 4, p. 2.

John Tierney, "New York's Parallel Lives," *New York Times Magazine,* 19 October 1997, sec. 6, p. 51.

Colon linking an elaboration

"The Birth of a New Species," in *Survey of the Software Industry* (insert), *The Economist* 339, no. 7967 (25 May 1996): 5.

The Economist, "We Know You're Reading This," *The Economist* 338, no. 7952 (10 February 1996): 27.

Robert Hughes, "American Visions," *Time,* special issue May 1997, 9.

John Tierney, "Let's Give Peace a Chance," *New York Times Magazine,* 2 November 1997, sec. 6, p. 30.

Parallel constructions

"We Know You're Reading This," *The Economist* 338, no. 7952 (10 February 1996): 28.

The World Development Report 1997: The State in a Changing World (New York: Oxford University Press, 1997), p. 20.

Book Currents, *New Yorker Magazine* 73, no. 38 (8 December 1997): 3.

Vladimir Nabokov, *Lectures on Literature* (1980; New York: Harcourt Brace Jovanovich, 1982), p. 3.

The verb-free element

Kevin Barry, "Still Clueless," *New York Times Book Review*, 7 December 1997, sec. 7, p. 46.

"The Next Revolution," in *Survey: Business in Eastern Europe, The Economist* 345, no. 8044 (22 November 1997): 3.

Edwin Dobb, "Where the Good Begins," *Harper's* 297, no. 1778 (July 1998): 60.

Elizabeth Cady Stanton, quoted in *The Norton Anthology of Literature by Women*, ed. Sandra M. Gilbert and Susan Gubar, 2d ed. (New York: Norton, 1996), p. 465.

9. ONE-SYLLABLE OPENINGS

It

André Gide, quoted in *Bartlett's Familiar Quotations*, 16th ed. (Boston: Little Brown, 1968), p. 607.

Paul Krugman, "Does Getting Old Cost Society Too Much?" *New York Times Magazine*, 9 March 1997, sec. 6, p. 60.

Richard Wright, *12 Million Black Voices* (New York: Viking, 1941), p. 101.

Henry R. Luce, *The American Century* (New York: Farrar and Rinehart, 1941), p. 22.

There

Ken Auletta, "Redstones Secret Weapon," *New Yorker Magazine* 70, no. 45 (16 January 1995): 51.

Michael Parfit, "Breathless," *New York Times Book Review*, 7 December 1997, sec. 7, p. 24.

Ian Blecher, Letters to the Editor, *New Yorker Magazine* 71, no. 22 (31 July 1995): 9.

"The End of the Miracle?" *The Economist* 345, no. 8047 (13 December 1997): 19.

This

William Safire, "Day of Infamy," *New York Times Magazine*, 7 December 1997, sec. 6, p. 30.

"Panic in South Korea," *The Economist* 345, no. 8047 (13 December 1997): 16.

"The End of the Miracle?" *The Economist* 345, no. 8047 (13 December 1997): 18.

Carol Lloyd, "Cents and Sensibility," *New York Times Magazine*, 28 December 1997, sec. 6, p. 50.

That

"The Kyoto Compromise," *The Economist* 345, no. 8047 (13 December 1997): 16.

"Drop That Steak or We Shoot," *The Economist* 345, no. 8047 (13 December 1997): 15.

"The End of the Miracle?" *The Economist* 345, no. 8047 (13 December 1997): 18.

Holly Brubach, "Doc Rotella's Cure for the Thinking Athlete," *New York Times Magazine*, 2 November 1997, sec. 6, p. 49.

What

"All This, and a Korean Election Too," *The Economist* 345, no. 8047 (13 December 1997): 34.

David Handelman, "The Ambivalent-about-Prime-Time Players," *New York Times Magazine* 28 December 1997, sec. 6, p. 28.

William Safire, "The Incredible 'n' Credible," *New York Times Magazine*, 28 December 1997, sec. 6, p. 10.

Joseph Epstein, "Portraits by Max," *New Yorker Magazine* 73, no. 38 (8 December 1997): 108–10.

EXEMPLARY SENTENCES

Clive Crook, "Europe's Gamble," in *The World in 1998* (a publication of *The Economist*) pp. 11–32.

Michiko Kakutani, "Master of His Domain," *New York Times Magazine*, 1 February 1998, sec. 6, p. 20.